nabokov.

nabokov
Live Theatre
HighTide Festival Theatre
in association with The North Wall
present the world premiere of

INCOGNITO

by Nick

D1639069

Incognito had its world premiere
on 12 April 2014 at the HighTide Festival, Suffolk,
with original cast Paul Hickey, Amelia Lowdell,
Alison O'Donnell and Sargon Yelda.

Incognito was originally commissioned
by Live Theatre and nabokov.

This production was supported by Arts Council England.

Supported using public funding by
ARTS COUNCIL
LOTTERY FUNDED | **ENGLAND**

Cast

in alphabetical order

Paul Hickey

Amelia Lowdel

Alison O'Donnell

Sargon Yelda

Creative and Production Team

Nick Payne	Writer
Joe Murphy	Director
Paul Jellis	Producer
Oliver Townsend	Designer
Tim Deiling	Lighting Designer
Isobel Waller-Bridge	Music and Sound
Hayley Kaimakliotis CDG	Casting Director
Lou Duffy	Costume Supervisor
Haruka Kuroda	Fight Director
Helen Ashton	Dialect Coach
Drummond Orr	Production Manager
Kate Schofield	Company Stage Manager
Naomi Lee	Deputy Stage Manager
Hannah Joss	Assistant Director

PAUL JELLIS – Producer
Paul Jellis is the Executive Producer of nabokov. Productions for nabokov include *Blink* by Phil Porter (Traverse, Soho Theatre, Jagriti Theatre Bangalore, UK tour, 59E59 New York), *Symphony* by Ella Hickson, Nick Payne and Tom Wells (Lyric Hammersmith, Outdoor Festivals Tour, VAULT festival) and *Fairy Tales* by Jack Thorne and Arthur Darvill (Latitude, BAC). He also programmes and produces nabokov's signature event *The nabokov Arts Club*. Paul is also a founder of interactive company Bad Physics. Productions for Bad Physics include *The Adventure* by Oliver Birch (HighTide Festival, Edinburgh Fringe, Royal Exchange Manchester), *The Enchanted Story Trail* by Joel Horwood (RHS Wisley), *Toad* by Dan Bird (Southwark Playhouse) and *Sunday Morning at the Centre of the World* (Southwark Playhouse, Brighton Fringe, BAC). Freelance work includes the European Première of *Gruesome Playground Injuries* by Rajiv Joseph (Gate Theatre). Paul is an Artistic Associate of HighTide Festival Theatre. www.pauljellis.co.uk

OLIVER TOWNSEND – Designer
Oliver Townsend trained at at RWCMD. He is an Artistic Associate at the Gate Theatre, Notting Hill. Set and costume designs include *Jack and The Beanstalk* (Lyric Hammersmith), *No Place to Go* (Gate), *The Blackest Black* (Hampstead), *Rodelinda* (Scottish Opera), *Grounded* (Gate Theatre; awarded Best Production and Best Set Designer at the 2013 Off West End Awards and a Fringe First at the 2013 Edinburgh Festival), *Macbeth* (Blackheath Halls Opera), *Hitchcock Blonde* (Hull Truck), *Blood Wedding* (Royal and Derngate), *Gods are Fallen and All Safety Gone* (Greyscale, Almeida Festival), *The Merchant of Venice* (Creation Theatre), *Wittenberg* (Gate). Costume designs include *The Measures Taken* (Alexander Whitley Dance Company, ROH Linbury), *Wozzeck* (English National Opera), *The Lighthouse* (English Touring Opera, ROH Linbury), and *Big Maggie* (Druid Theatre). www.oftownsend.co.uk

TIM DEILING – Lighting Designer
Tim Deiling's theatre credits include *HMS Pinafore* (Hackney Empire), *BARE* (Greenwich Theatre), *Pipe Dream*, *BARE*, *and Billy* (The Union), *Good With People* (59E59, NYC), *The 8th* (Barbican), *Wigan, 65 Miles* (Hull Truck), *The Last Days of Judas Iscariot* (Platform Theatre), *Chips with Everything* (Embassy Studio), the UK premiere of *Back of the Throat* (Old Red Lion Theatre), *The Oikos Project*, *Protozoa* (The Red Room), *Zombie Prom The Musical* (Landor Theatre), *Macbeth* (Sprite Productions), *Boiling Frogs* (Factory Theatre). He is resident lighting designer at The Box, Soho, and co-lit eleven new plays for *The Broken Space*

Season (Bush). Tim is Associate Lighting Designer for the National Theatre. Credits as Assistant Lighting Designer include *Scottsboro Boys* (Young Vic*)*, *Chicago* (UK Tour, China, Madrid, Spanish Tour, Seoul), *9 to 5 The Musical* (UK Tour), *Pippin* (Chocolate Factory), and *High School Musical 2* (UK Tour). Film credits include lighting *Animal Charm*, *The Actress*, and *Suzie Luvitt* for Ben Edwards and *The Prank Show* for the BBC. Tim also received the Young Lighting Designer of the Year award from the Association of Lighting Designers in 2008.
www.TimDeiling.com

ISOBEL WALLER-BRIDGE – Music and Sound
Isobel Waller-Bridge trained at Edinburgh University, Kings College London and the Royal Academy of Music. Theatre credits as composer include *King Lear* (Chichester Festival Theatre, BAM New York), *Neville's Island* (Chichester Festival Theatre), *If Only* (Minerva Theatre). Credits as composer and sound designer include *Incognito* (HighTide Festival, Bush Theatre), *Orlando* (Manchester Royal Exchange), *Fleabag* (Soho Theatre), *Yellow Face* (Park Theatre, The NT Shed), *Forever House* (Theatre Royal Plymouth), *Sleuth* (Watermill Theatre), *Gruesome Playground Injuries* (Gate Theatre), *Mydidae* (Soho Theatre and Trafalgar Studios), *Blink* (Traverse Theatre and Soho Theatre) and *The Girl with the Iron Claws* (Arcola Theatre); as musical director, *A Woman Killed with Kindness* (National Theatre) and *A Christmas Carol* (Library Theatre Manchester); as music associate and musician, *The Children's Hour* (Comedy Theatre), *Rocket to the Moon* and *Welcome to Thebes* (National Theatre). Television, film and radio credits as composer include *Secret Symphony* (Samsung, Times), *Gilead* (Radio 3), *Physics* (Winner Best Short BFI Film Festival 2013), *Ellie*, *Disaffected*, *Beautiful Enough*, *Hometown* and *Meeting Mr Tiller;* as orchestrator/arranger, *The Imposter* (BAFTA winner), *Life* (Ivor Novello winner), *Planet Earth Live!*, *The Bounty Hunter*, *The Day of the Flowers* and *Route Irish.* As musical director, *The Boy I Love* (V&A Films). www.isobelwaller-bridge.com

HANNAH JOSS – Assistant Director
Hannah Joss trained in theatre directing at Mountview Academy of Theatre Arts. Credits as director include *That Moment* (Crescent Arts Centre, Belfast, RADA), *Talking to Alice* (Old Vic New Voices), *Rapid-WriteResponse: Polythene* (Theatre 503), *The Teenagers* (Theatre Delicatessen), *The Man with the Heart of a Pig* (Old Red Lion), *The Devil Inside Him* (The White Bear), *It Felt Empty When the Heart Went at First but it is Alright Now* (Cockpit Theatre). Credits as assistant director include *Henry V* (Theatre Delicatessen), *Dracula* (Leicester Square Theatre). Hannah directs sketch comedy group *Mixed Doubles*, who are soon to appear on BBC Radio 4.

nabokov.

nabokov is a theatre company based in the eastern region, dedicated to putting new writing at the heart of British culture.

Through a pioneering commissioning and creative process we challenge writers and audiences to re-invent how new writing is made and experienced.

Since 2001 nabokov has hosted an extraordinarily diverse programme around the UK and internationally, premiering the work of over 1,000 artists. We have produced and curated vibrant artistic events at venues and festivals around the country, as well as touring premiere flagship productions.

Previous productions include the world premieres of *Blink* by Phil Porter (Traverse, Soho Theatre, Jagriti Theatre Bangalore, UK tour, 59E59 Theaters New York); *Symphony*, a theatre/live music collaboration with composer Ed Gaughan and writers Ella Hickson, Nick Payne and Tom Wells (Lyric Hammersmith, Greenwich+Docklands International Festival, Imagine Watford, Latitude, VAULT Festival); *Young Pretender* by EV Crowe (Underbelly, UK tour); the Fringe First winning *Bunny* by Jack Thorne (Underbelly, Soho Theatre, UK Tour, 59E59 New York); *Fairy Tales* by Jack Thorne and Arthur Darvill (Latitude, BAC); *Is Everyone OK?* by Joel Horwood (Latitude Festival, Drum Theatre Plymouth, UK Tour); *2nd May 1997* by Jack Thorne (Bush Theatre, UK tour); *Artefacts* by Mike Bartlett (Bush Theatre, UK tour, 59E59 New York); and *Terre Haute* by Edmund Whlte (Trafalgar Studios, UK Tour, 59E59 New York).

Ours is a writer-led theatre that embraces all the innovation, complexity and diversity of the twenty-first century.

nabokov staff

Artistic Director – Joe Murphy
Executive Producer – Paul Jellis
Executive Director – Ric Mountjoy
General Manager – Corinne Salisbury
Advisory Board – Emma Brunjes, James Grieve,
George Perrin, Imogen Kinchin, Mike Bartlett

nabokov is an associate company of Watford Palace Theatre and Soho Theatre and is project funded by Arts Council England.

live
theatre

Live Theatre is one of the UK's leading new writing theatres. From its base on Newcastle's quayside, Live Theatre produces work as varied and diverse as the audiences it engages with. Live Theatre creates and performs new plays of world class quality, finds and develops creative talent and unlocks the potential of young people through theatre. Last year Live Theatre celebrated forty years of making plays, on Tyneside, but also nationally and internationally.

Transformed in 2007 with a capital redevelopment, the Theatre is in complex of beautifully restored Grade II listed buildings with state-of-the-art facilities in a unique historical setting, including a 160-seat cabaret-style theatre, a studio theatre, renovated rehearsal rooms, dedicated writer's rooms as well as a thriving café, bar and pub.

Live Theatre has just announced LiveWorks, a £10 million capital development to purchase and develop Quayside-fronted land and buildings adjacent to the Theatre, to create new commercial office space, a new public park and a children and young people's writing centre.

Live Theatre is a national leader in developing new strategies for developing income and assets for the charity. LiveWorks will join The Broad Chare pub, online playwriting course www.beaplaywright.com and The Schoolhouse (an office space for SMEs), as one of Live Theatre's creative enterprises, which increases funds through new income streams.

For more information see
www.live.org.uk

Best Friends

Noreen Bates, Jim Beirne, Michael & Pat Brown, Paul Callaghan, George Caulkin, Mauyra Cushlow, Michael & Susan Chaplin, Helen Coyne, Robson Green, Lee Hall, John Jordan, John Josephs, Annette Marlowe, Madelaine Newton, Elaine Orrick, Elaine Sandy, Ian & Christine Shepherdson, Margaret & John Shipley, Shelagh Stephenson, Sting, Peter Straughan, Paul & Julie Tomlinson, Nick & Melanie Tulip, Alison Walton, Kevin Whately and Lucy Winskell

Supported using public funding by
ARTS COUNCIL ENGLAND

Newcastle
City Council

Live Theatre Staff

Jim Beirne – Chief Executive
Max Roberts – Artistic Director
Wendy Barnfather – Operations Director
Lucy Bird – Director of Enterprise & Development
Clare Overton – Administrator, Directors

Catherine Moody – Finance Officer (Maternity Leave)
Helen Tuffnell – Finance Assistant (Maternity Cover)
Nicole Huddart – Finance Assistant

Cait Read – Marketing Manager
Claire Cockroft – Marketing Manager
Emma Hall – Marketing & Press Officer
Melanie Rashbrooke – Marketing & Press Assistant
Amy Foley – Box Office Administrator

Helen Moore – Director Of Education & Engagement
Paul James – Associate Director
Philip Hoffmann – Drama Worker
Rachel Glover – Drama Worker
Sam Bell – Administrator

Steve Gilroy – Associate Director
Graeme Thompson – Creative Producer
Degna Stone – Administrator
Gez Casey – Literary Manager

Drummond Orr – Production Manager
Dave Flynn – Technical Manager
Hannah Gregory – Technician
Craig Spence – Technical Apprentice

Carole Wears – House Manager
Michael Davies – Deputy House Manager
Ben Young – Duty House Manager
Mark Gerrens – Duty House Manager

Box Office and Front of House staff
Nina Berry, Chris Foley, Lewis Jobson, Caroline Liversidge,
Sarah Matthews, Emily Merritt, Hannah Murphy, Charlotte Kell,
Tilly Riley, Molly Wright, Camille Burridge, Meghan Doyle ,
Danielle Burn, Clare Overton, Helen Tuffnell, Nicole Huddart
and Chris Foley

HighTide Festival Theatre

Makers of New Theatre

"One of the little gems of the artistic calendar in Britain" The Telegraph

"Famous for championing emerging playwrights and contemporary theatre" Daily Mail

HighTide Festival Theatre is one of the UK's leading producers of new plays, and the only professional theatre focused on the production of new playwrights. Currently we read and consider around 1000 scripts a year from around the world, from which we then work with 100 playwrights on a range of development opportunities, from workshops to full productions. Every play that we receive is read by our Artistic Director and Associates.

Under Steven Atkinson, co-founding Artistic Director, we have premièred major productions by playwrights including Ella Hickson, Frances Ya-Chu Cowhig, Nick Payne, Adam Brace, Beth Steel, Laura Poliakoff, Luke Barnes, Vickie Donoghue, Lydia Adetunji, Jack Thorne and Joel Horwood. We produce several productions a year in our annual Suffolk festival and on tour.

In seven years we have staged over fifty productions, producing new work with some of the world's leading theatres in London (including the National Theatre, Bush Theatre, Old Vic Theatre and Soho Theatre), regionally (including Sheffield Theatres, Watford Palace and Theatre Royal Bath) and internationally (In New York 59E59 and the Public Theater, and in Australia the National Play Festival).

Lansons host our administrative offices in-kind within their Clerkenwell offices. This innovative partnership between a business and charity has won five Corporate Engagement Awards, a Social Impact Award, an Arts & Business award nomination, and has been profiled by the Guardian and the Evening Standard.

HighTide Festival Theatre is a National Portfolio Organisation of Arts Council England.

Image: **Boys** by Ella Hickson (HighTide 2012)
Photographer: Bill Knight

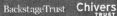

Incognito

Nick Payne's *If There Is I Haven't Found It Yet* was staged at the Bush Theatre in 2009 and went on to receive that year's George Devine Award. His next play, *Wanderlust*, opened at the Royal Court in 2010. *One Day When We Were Young*, in a Paines Plough and Sheffield Theatres co-production, was staged at the Crucible Studio Theatre, Sheffield, in 2011, and later transferred to Shoreditch Town Hall. *Constellations*, which opened at the Royal Court in 2012 and transferred to the Duke of York's Theatre, won the Evening Standard Theatre Award for Best Play. *The Same Deep Water As Me* was staged at the Donmar Warehouse in 2013 and received an Olivier Award nomination for Best New Comedy.

also by Nick Payne from Faber

IF THERE IS I HAVEN'T FOUND IT YET
WANDERLUST
ONE DAY WHEN WE WERE YOUNG
CONSTELLATIONS
THE SAME DEEP WATER AS ME

NICK PAYNE

Incognito

FABER & FABER

First published in 2014
by Faber and Faber Ltd
74–77 Great Russell Street
London WC1B 3DA

Reprinted with revisions, May 2014

Typeset by Country Setting, Kingsdown, Kent CT14 8ES
Printed in England by CPI Group (UK) Ltd, Croydon CR0 4YY

A CIP record for this book is available from the British Library

978–0–571–31707–3

2 4 6 8 10 9 7 5 3

Acknowledgements

Steven Atkinson, Remy Beasley, British Association for Adoption and Fostering, British Neuropsychological Society, Gez Casey, Paul Broks, Lisa Claydon, Paul Hickey, Paul Jellis, Miranda Julia, Professor Narinder Kapur, Amelia Lowdell, Denise McCartan, Joe Murphy, Alison O'Donnell, David Ormerod, Max Roberts, John Rumbold, Karen Shaw and Susan Stoneham of the Queen Square Brain Bank for Neurological Disorders, Professor Barbara Wilson and Sargon Yelda

Ben Hall and Lily Williams at Curtis Brown, and John Buzzetti at WME

Minna

Mum

Lastly, I would like to acknowledge the following books and their authors: *Possessing Genius: The Bizarre Odyssey of Einstein's Brain* by Carolyn Abraham, *Into the Silent Land* by Paul Broks, *Permanent Present Tense* by Suzanne Corkin, *Incognito* by David Eagleman, *Moonwalking with Einstein: The Art and Science of Remembering Everything* by Joshua Foer, *The Paradoxical Brain* edited by Narinder Kapur, *The Time Traveller* by Ronald L. Mallett, *Driving Mr Albert: A Trip Across American with Einstein's Brain* by Michael Paterniti, *The Making of Memory: From Molecules to Mind* by Steven Rose, *Forever Today: A Memoir of Love and Amnesia* by Deborah Wearing and *Case Studies in Neuropsychological Rehabilitation* by Barbara Wilson.

Despite being based, albeit very loosely, on several true stories, this play is a work of fiction. But then isn't everything.

What binds that me to this me, and allows me to maintain the illusion that there is continuity from moment to moment and year to year, is some relatively stable but gradually evolving thing at the nucleus of my being. Call it a soul, or a self, or an emergent by-product of a neural network, but whatever you want to call it, that element of continuity is entirely dependent on memory.

Joshua Foer, *Moonwalking with Einstein:*
The Art and Science of Remembering Everything
(London: Penguin Books, 2011), p. 86

In order to survive, humans have invented science. Pursued consistently, scientific enquiry acts to undermine myth. But life without myth is impossible, so science has become a channel for myths – chief among them, a myth of salvation through science.

John Gray, *The Silence of Animals*
(London: Allen Lane, 2013), p. 82

Who tells the story of the self? That's like asking who thunders the thunder or rains the rain. It is not so much a question of us telling the story as the story telling us.

Paul Broks, *Into the Silent Land*
(London: Atlantic Books, 2004), p. 41

Characters

Thomas Stoltz Harvey
born in Kansas, USA, 1912

Elouise Harvey
born in New York, USA, 1912

Hans Albert Einstein
born in Bern, Switzerland, 1904

Lisa-Scott Hannigan
born in Sydney, Australia, *c.* 1941

Freddy Myers
twenties

Anna Vann
thirties

Michael Wolf
born in Maine, USA, *c.* 1965

Otto Nathan
born in Bigen, Germany, 1893

Evelyn Einstein
born in Chicago, USA, 1941

Henry Maison
born in Bath, UK, 1933

Margaret Thomson
born in Bath, UK, 1933

Victor Milner
born in Hertfordshire, UK, *c.* 1913

Jon Williams
born in Cardiff, UK, forties

Sharon Shaw
forties

Martha Murphy
born in London, UK, 1971

Patricia Thorn
born in London, UK, *c.* 1978

'Anthony'
forties

Richard Walsh
fifties

Brenda Walsh
fifties

Ben Murphy
early twenties

Greg Barraclough
thirties

Doubling

Male, forties: Thomas Harvey, Victor Milner,
'Anthony', Richard Walsh, Jon Williams, Otto Nathan

Female, forties: Martha Murphy, Elouise Harvey,
Brenda Walsh, Anna Vann, Evelyn Einstein

Female, twenties to thirties: Margaret Thomson,
Lisa-Scott Hannigan, Patricia Thorn, Sharon Shaw

Male, twenties to thirties: Henry Maison, Michael Wolf,
Hans Albert Einstein, Ben Murphy, Freddy Myers,
Greg Barraclough

INCOGNITO

For Dad

Encoding

Michael Evelyn?

Evelyn Excuse me?

Michael My name is Michael, Michael Wolf? I wrote you a coupla months back –

Evelyn I have nothing to say to you.

Michael If I can have, like, two minutes –

Evelyn I don't appreciate being followed.

Michael What? No, oh my God; that is so not what this is about –

Evelyn I got your letters, Michael, and you wanna know what I did with them?

Michael Can I like –

Evelyn I fed them to my poodle.

Michael Look, I get why the whole me-approaching-you-in-the-street thing is kinda unorthodox –

Evelyn Goodbye, Michael.

Michael I think I know who your father is. I think I know who your father is. And if you can gimme, like, five minutes of your –

Evelyn Excuse me?

Michael I . . . think I know who your father is.

Beat.

Evelyn Five minutes?

Michael Five minutes.

Evelyn I have an appointment.

Michael Got it.

Evelyn I have an ulcer.

Michael I'm sorry to hear that.

Evelyn Needs looking at.

Michael Got it.

Evelyn The clock is ticking, Michael.

Michael Okay, so there is like, *so* much I wanna . . . You know about the professor's executor, right?

Evelyn I know he died, if that's what you mean.

Michael Right. Well it turned out this guy, this Otto Nathan guy, had been sitting on this, like, goldmine of like – I mean letters and diaries and correspondences – 'bout the professor. And I mean some of these letters, I mean some of these, like, *exchanges*, no one, and I mean not one goddamn person, had ever . . . Otto had this like whole library of these, like –

Evelyn Three minutes, Michael.

Michael I think the professor had an affair with a ballet dancer. When he was sixty-two, I think the professor had an affair with a ballet dancer from the New York Ballet, and I think Otto knew about it and I think he kept the whole thing a secret – And I'm sorry if this is literally like the crudest summation of your life, like, ever, but –

Evelyn Final minute.

Michael Evelyn, Hans Albert wasn't your father, and I know you maybe kinda already know 'bout that, but what

14

I mean is – Hans Albert was your brother and the . . .
I am like ninety-nine-per-cent certain that the professor
was your father. And I know what you're probably
thinking –

Evelyn I very much doubt that.

Michael Why in the hell should I trust a reporter, right?

Evelyn Time's up.

Michael Evelyn, there's this guy, there's this guy named
Thomas Harvey –

Evelyn Don't ever come to my street again.

Michael Evelyn, Evelyn –

Evelyn I have an appointment and I gave you your five
minutes, Michael, and I would be grateful –

Michael Harvey took the professor's brain – And I think
he still has it and I think you could do a DNA test. You
could find out. If I can find this guy, and I think that I
can, Evelyn – you could use the brain to perform a DNA
test, and you could know for sure, who you are, one way
or the other. (*Beat.*) Milk. My mom used to say you gotta
drink a glass and a half of milk. Ulcers.

    Beat.

Listen, can I buy you lunch?

Victor Hello Henry.

Henry Hello.

Margaret Hello Henry.

Henry Hello my love, where have you been?

Margaret Right here. I've been right here.

Henry I thought you'd left?

Margaret No.

Henry Where have you been?

Margaret I've been right here.

Henry Well, it's good to see you.

Margaret You too.

Victor Did you have a good night's sleep, Henry?

Henry Tell you the truth, I didn't stay awake to find out.

Victor Now, Henry, Margaret tells me you're quite the piano player? Margaret tells me you're a bit of a *dab hand.*

Henry I don't know . . .

Victor What do you think, Henry; would you like to give it a go?

Victor gestures to a piano. Henry moves to the piano and takes a seat.

Henry What do you want me to play?

Margaret Whatever you want.

Henry (*beat*) I'm not sure I know how to?

Margaret You do. I promise you.

She takes a seat beside Henry.

Victor We have to let him –

Margaret I know. (*Beat.*) Ready?

Henry As I'll ever be.

Margaret plays a note. Beat, then:
Henry plays the same note but not quite as well.

Victor The idea is to let him –

Margaret I know.

Victor Margaret, I understand this is difficult for you –

Margaret Please.

> *Beat. Margaret plays a different note. Henry mimics.*
> *Margaret plays a different note. Henry mimics.*
> *Margaret plays a very brief, straightforward melody.*

Henry . . .

Margaret Henry?

Henry Hello my love, where have you been?

Margaret (*beat, then*) Here. I've been right here.

Victor Perhaps we ought to stop?

Patricia Martha?

Martha Yes.

Patricia Patricia.

Martha How's it going?

Patricia I'm sorry I'm so late.

Martha You're not that late.

Patricia I'm pretty late.

Martha You are pretty late, but that's alright.

Patricia Are you angry?

Martha No.

Patricia You sound sort of angry?

Martha This is how I normally sound.

Patricia Then we ought to get you a drink, angry lady.

Martha The bar was pretty busy.

Patricia They normally come and take your order.

Martha There weren't any tables.

Patricia I'm still getting the angry voice, gotta be honest.

Martha Sorry – You're right. I am annoyed. I'm sorry. I got here, on time, about half an hour ago, and the place was rammed, full of fucking hipsters, no seats, and when I tried getting served, tried to actually order a drink, nobody seemed remotely interested, so I stood around for a while, pretending to check my emails, then I went to the loo, *then*, for no discernible reason whatsoever, I listened to a load of old voicemails, and then I came outside for a cigarette even though I'm trying to quit.

Patricia And then I arrived – 'Yay'. I am really fucking sorry. I'm serious.

Martha It's okay.

Patricia It's not.

Martha It's not, but in the grand scheme of things it is.

Patricia I got made redundant. Like, a week ago. And I went in, today, to see a colleague, and I had like this total fucking meltdown. I got really sad, I went home, I smoked a joint and I may or may not have had a small helping of Bombay Sapphire after which I may or may not have fallen asleep, woken up, looked at my watch and gone – (*whispers*) 'Fuuuuck'.

Martha I'm sorry to hear about your job.

Patricia Yeah well, you know what? Fuck 'em. But enough about me, let's talk about me. D'you wanna go somewhere else?

Martha I really don't mind either way.

Patricia Be honest.

Martha I really am sorry to hear about your job.

Patricia Thank you.

Martha But yes, this place is my idea of hell.

Patricia Then let's ditch these fucking hipsters and go and eat some burgers.

Martha I'm vegan.

Patricia Then let's ditch these fucking hipsters and go and eat some tofu and mung beans.

Martha Am I allowed to have one more cigarette?

Patricia How serious are you about tryina quit?

Beat.

I'm s'posed to be doing this five–two diet?

Martha How's that going?

Patricia On the two days, I literally fucking wanna kill myself, but on the five days, I just eat cake on the hour every hour. In many ways it's the perfect balance.

Martha offers Patricia a cigarette.

No thank you. So how long have you been vegan, Martha?

Martha Since I was a teenager. My parents, adoptive parents, were vegans.

Patricia Have you ever cracked?

Martha I had bacon once.

Patricia That's it?

Martha That's it.

Patricia That's a pretty fucking solid track record.

Martha I went through a phase of eating fish when I was at university.

Patricia I knew it.

Martha Why are you on a diet?

Patricia Because, well, here's the thing: I registered with a new GP, I moved flats recently, and when you register you have to do the whole nurse thing where they weigh you, right? And the nurse said I was seven kilograms overweight and I was like: could it be my shoes?

Martha And she said . . .

Patricia 'Young lady, those shoes are the least of your worries.' Can I make a confession?

Martha Okay.

Patricia Even though I pretended I understood your job, when we were emailing, I actually didn't. And I googled UCL and everything.

Martha I'm a clinical neuropsychologist.

Patricia Brilliant, because, I was just saying to a friend last week, if there is one thing we are short of in this world . . .

Martha I run the Neuropsychology Department.

Patricia Wow, you're proper.

Martha I wish.

Patricia (*cigarette*) Don't feel you have to rush that, by the way.

Martha Okay. (*Finishes her cigarette. Beat.*) Done.

Patricia Ready?

Elouise Where on earth have you been?

Harvey Elouise –

Elouise I called the hospital –

Harvey Honey –

Elouise The boys and I have been –

Harvey Honey, something real big happened at work today.

Elouise Well, I should hope so –

Harvey No, I mean real big.

Elouise (*beat*) Well, are you gonna tell me or am I gonna have to –

Harvey Albert Einstein passed away.

Elouise What?

Harvey You remember I told you he came inna the hospital a couple of weeks back and we took some blood and urine?

Elouise Yuh-huh.

Harvey This morning I got a call from Jack who just got off the phone with Guy Dean. The professor suffered an aneurysm overnight and they couldn't stop the bleeding. The professor's son, a fella named Hans Albert –

Elouise Beautiful name.

Harvey You think?

Elouise I really do.

Harvey I think it's kinda austere.

Elouise It's a beautiful name.

Harvey Anyway: Hans Albert wants Jack to perform the autopsy, but Jack's away in –

Elouise Vermont.

Harvey Right. So Jack calls me and he says: 'Harve, you gotta do this.'

Elouise Oh. My. God.

Harvey So I get outta bed –

Elouise Why didn't you mention none of this this morning?

Harvey There wasn't time to get into it.

Elouise So what happened when you made it to the hospital?

Harvey When I get there, I'm introduced to this fella named Otto Nathan.

Elouise German?

Harvey Maybe.

Elouise Otto.

Harvey Right.

Elouise Otto Nathan.

Harvey He's the professor's executor. Wants to meet me. Says he wants to watch.

Elouise Watch?

Harvey The autopsy.

Elouise That is not normal.

Harvey Fella seems kinda normal to me.

Elouise Who watches autopsies?

Harvey He's distraught.

22

Elouise It ain't right.

Harvey Honey, honey: here's the thing.

Elouise What's the thing?

Harvey He –

Elouise Tell me what the thing is.

Harvey He wants me to speak to the press first thing tomorrow morning.

Elouise Oh. My. God.

Harvey Could be a helluva crowd.

Elouise I gotta call Ma.

Harvey No.

Elouise What?

Harvey She hasta read about it in the news like everybody else.

Elouise When she reads about it in the news, you know what she's gonna think? She's gonna think how come I ain't heard about this already. And you know what she's gonna do then?

Harvey There's something else.

Elouise What?

Harvey Something else I gotta tell ya.

Elouise (*beat*) What'd you do?

Harvey I was, I was looking at this fella, right? One of the greatest minds of the twentieth century, right, no question. And he's pale. And he's kinda small. Fragile-looking, okay, kinda small and kinda fragile-looking. And I say to Otto, I say: you got any kinda studies lined up? And he looks at me and I say: studies, you know, scientific? This is the brain of a genius, right, it oughta be studied.

Elouise Thomas Harvey –

Harvey Just lemme . . .! So I ask about the will. I say there's gotta be something in the professor's will, right? The fella's clueless. Anyway, the point – I got the professor in fronta me, I already opened him up and I'm looking at this . . . brain, and I'm thinking to myself: this could be the biggest moment of my life. So I took it.

Elouise The moment?

Harvey The brain.

Elouise What?

Harvey I took the brain.

Elouise You took Albert Einstein's brain –

Harvey Exactly.

Elouise You took Albert Einstein's brain, are you kidding me?!

Harvey Honey –

Elouise Is that even legal?

Harvey Of course it is. I'm a pathologist.

Elouise You're seriously tryina tell me –

Harvey I took the brain.

Elouise What'd you do with it?

Harvey It's in the trunk of the car.

Elouise Sweet mother of –

Harvey Elouise, you gotta calm down.

Elouise In the trunk of the car, are you kidding me?

Harvey I didn't wanna leave it at the hospital.

Elouise Well, you gotta give it back.

Harvey I'm gonna speak to Hans Albert.

Elouise Thomas Harvey –

Harvey Listen: I'm gonna speak to Hans Albert and I'm gonna straighten this whole thing out.

Elouise I need a drink.

Victor Hello Henry.

Margaret Hello Henry.

Henry Hello my love, where have you been?

Margaret Right here. I've been right here.

Henry I thought you'd left?

Margaret No.

Henry Well, it's good to see you.

Margaret You too.

Victor Did you have a good night's sleep, Henry?

Henry Tell you the truth, I didn't stay awake to find out.

Margaret Henry?

Henry Yes, my love.

Margaret I was wondering if you might be able to play something on the piano for Dr Milner?

Henry . . .

Margaret Henry.

Henry Hello my love, where have you been?

Margaret Here, I am always here.

Henry I thought you'd left?

Margaret Henry, please listen to me.

Henry It's good to see you, my love.

Margaret Henry, please!

Victor Perhaps we ought to leave it there?

Margaret Henry, Dr Milner and I would like to hear you play the piano.

Henry Alright.

Margaret Now, Henry.

Henry I might be a bit rusty.

Margaret It doesn't matter.

Henry moves to the piano and takes a seat.

Henry (*beat*) I'm not sure I know how to?

Margaret You do. I promise you.

Beat. Margaret takes a seat beside Henry.

Victor Margaret, I know this is difficult, but we –

Margaret (*to Henry*) Ready?

Henry As I'll ever be.

Margaret (*beat*) Henry, please.

Henry plays a note.

Margaret That's it.

Henry plays a different note.

That's it.

Henry plays a different note. Beat. Plays a few more notes; he's nearly playing a melody. Beat.

Henry?

Henry Hello my love, where have you been?

Margaret shoves or pushes Henry out of sheer frustration. This frightens Henry.

I don't understand?

Margaret I'm sorry. I'm sorry, I . . .

Margaret kisses Henry softly on the lips.

Victor Thank you, Henry. I'll think we'll stop there.

Martha Morning.

Patricia Hello Martha.

Martha How are you?

Patricia I think I'm pretty terrifically hungover.

Martha Same. (*Beat.*) Was I sick?

Patricia A little bit.

Martha You can say.

Patricia You were pretty sick.

Martha Sick-in-here sick, or sick-somewhere-else sick?

Patricia A mix of outside and in.

Martha I'm so sorry. Did you have to clean up?

Patricia I thought it was the ladylike thing to do.

Martha What did you use?

Patricia I used some towels.

Martha Towels plural?

Patricia Yeah.

Martha How many towels plural?

Patricia Three.

Martha I was sick on three towels?

Patricia You weren't strictly speaking sick on the towels, no. But, yes, the towels were the main cleaning implement used to dispense of the sick.

Martha Whereabouts?

Patricia A combination of the bathroom and ze landing.

Martha Christ. I am so –

Patricia It's totally fine.

Martha It's not.

Patricia It really is.

Martha Thank you for looking after me. In my own home no less. (*Beat.*) I have to go to work now.

Patricia Okay – When d'you, when d'you need to – Can I have, like, ten minutes –

Martha You can stay. If you wanted.

Patricia Oh.

Martha Help yourself to some. Bran Flakes. If you like.

Patricia Oh, okay.

Martha Or go. If you – I can –

Patricia No, it's a two-day, so Bran Flakes would be, fucking, bang on.

Martha There's a spare key, also, if you wanted to come and go.

Patricia Wow.

Martha Or not.

Patricia No, that's –

Martha I'll be back around sevenish.

Patricia Okay.

Martha But if you need to go –

Patricia I'm redundant, so.

Martha I have Netflix.

Patricia Nice.

Martha If you – I don't know – If you didn't feel like – If you felt like a day in front of the –

Patricia Netflix sounds epic.

Martha I ought to go.

Patricia I ought to have some Bran Flakes.

Martha There's my mobile and my direct line, just in case.

Patricia Okay.

Martha Only just in case.

Patricia Your secret's safe with me.

Martha What?

Patricia Have a really good day at work.

Martha Yes. I'm really sorry again you had to clear up my sick.

Patricia It's the towels you ought to be apologising to.

Martha Have a good day.

Patricia Yes.

Martha Bye.

Patricia Bye.

Martha Bye.

Harvey (*to Hans Albert*) It's a real pleasure to meet you, sir. This is my wife, Elouise.

Elouise Pleased to meet you, Mr . . . Einstein?

Hans A. You can call me Hans, if you like; it's a bit more straightforward.

Elouise Hans. I gotta tell you, you got a great name.

Hans A. Thank you, Mrs Harvey.

Elouise Will you be staying for dinner, Hans?

Hans A. No thank you, Mrs Harvey, I don't think so.

Elouise There's meatloaf.

Hans A. I wish I could oblige but my appetite has been somewhat diminished of late.

Elouise I can't begin to imagine what you must have been through. I was very sorry to hear of your father's passing.

Hans A. Thank you.

Elouise Can we offer you something to drink?

Hans A. Oh, no thank you.

Harvey How was the journey from California, Mr Einstein?

Elouise Hans.

Hans A. Long, sadly.

Harvey I'm sorry to hear that. (*Beat.*) Well. Thank you for coming to see us this evening. (*Beat, nervously kicking things off.*) Sir, I wish to study your father's brain. I believe there could be great, untold scientific value in doing so. Furthermore, if you entrust your father's brain to me, not only will I take great care of it, I will ensure that it will be neither exploited or exposed to adverse publicity. Any research findings will appear only in accredited, scientific journals. (*Beat.*) That's it. That's my pitch.

Elouise Honey, don't call it a pitch.

Hans A. I can't pretend I wasn't a little distressed when I heard that you had removed my father's brain, Mr Harvey.

Harvey And I –

Elouise Let the man speak.

Harvey Sorry.

Hans A. (*'thank you'*) Mrs Harvey. I have spent my life living in my father's shadow, Mr Harvey. Perhaps I ought to feel outraged, as some do, at what you have done. But I don't. My father was a strange, often cruel individual and I –

Harvey I'm sorry to hear that.

Elouise Honey.

Harvey Sorry.

Hans A. If you truly wish to study my father's brain then I am happy to grant you permission to do so. But I wish to have no part in it.

Harvey I understand. Thank you. I think this could be the start of something really spectacular, real important.

Elouise How long will you be in New Jersey for, Hans?

Hans A. A week or so.

Elouise Do you have your family with you?

Hans A. Yes.

Elouise Two boys, is that right?

Hans A. And a daughter, that's correct. Bernhard, Klaus and Evelyn.

Elouise Beautiful names.

Hans A. We like to think so.

Elouise Sure you don't wanna take a little meatloaf for the family? I make a helluva meatloaf.

Hans A. I don't doubt it.

Harvey I can vouch for that.

Hans A. That's very kind of you, Mrs Harvey, but no thank you.

Elouise Call me Elouise.

Hans A. Mr Harvey, may I ask you a question?

Harvey Shoot.

Hans A. Do you have it here?

Harvey The brain?

Hans A. That's correct.

Harvey It's in the basement.

Hans A. The basement?

Harvey It's a matter of temperature. Not to mention safety.

Hans A. You're preserving it in some kind of solution, I presume?

Harvey You bet. I dissected the brain into two hundred and forty-two pieces –

Elouise Honey.

Harvey What?

Elouise Too much.

Hans A. I don't mind.

Harvey You wanna see it?

Elouise Of course he doesn't wanna –

Hans A. No thank you.

Harvey Lemme give you my card. You change your mind, maybe you, uh, maybe you wanna see it, anything, you just call that number right there. Anytime.

Hans A. Thank you.

Victor Hello Henry.

Henry Hello.

Margaret Hello Henry.

Henry Hello my love, where have you been?

Margaret I've been right here, Henry.

Henry It's good to see you.

Victor Henry, may I ask you a question?

Henry Please.

Victor Have we met before?

Henry Have . . .

Victor We met before.

Henry Not . . . not that I can recall. No.

Victor Henry, do you know where you are?

Henry I'm on my way home . . . Margaret and I went to . . . London. I am due to receive an operation, to alleviate my . . . seizures. And, then, once that's all done and dusted, Margaret and I will be able to take our . . . honeymoon.

Margaret Henry.

Henry Yes, my love.

Margaret Dr Milner and I were wondering if you might play us something on the piano?

Henry Alright.

Margaret Thank you, Henry.

Henry I might be a bit rusty.

Margaret You won't.

Henry moves to the piano and takes a seat. Beat.

Henry I'm not sure I know how to?

Margaret You do.

Beat.

Margaret (*takes a seat beside Henry*) I'll start you off.

She plays a note. Henry mimics, quickly and accurately. Henry now plays one or two more notes without Margaret's assistance.

That's it, Henry.

34

Henry plays a melody. It's a bit slow and bit ropey here and there, but nonetheless it's a complete melody for the first time. Henry falters and stops. Beat.

Henry, that was wonderful. Wasn't it?

Victor Yes. Thank you, Henry.

Margaret You see, he's –

Victor Yes.

Margaret He's improving.

Victor He is.

Margaret He's improving. You're improving.

Anthony Imagination is more important than knowledge. Knowledge is limited. Imagination encircles the world, do you know who said that?

Martha Who?

Anthony Einstein.

Martha I didn't know that.

Anthony Have I told you about Deborah?

Martha Anthony, would you mind if I ask you some questions?

Anthony Of course not.

Martha Great.

Anthony Have I told you about Deborah?

Martha . . .

Anthony I'm going to ask her to marry me. D'you wanna see the ring?

Martha If you want.

Anthony Must've left it somewhere.

Martha Anthony. Anthony –

Anthony Deborah's a physicist, have I told you about Deborah?

Martha You have.

Anthony D'you know how we met?

Martha I don't, no.

Anthony We met at York. Have you been to York?

Martha I haven't, no.

Anthony We met at a party. That's the good thing about the first year of undergraduate study, you get to interact with students from other subjects. I guess maybe later on there's no need to, to interact with other subjects. Deborah was at the party, I went outside because I'm not, I'm not really a fan of small spaces. I was with everyone, in the kitchen. I went outside to smoke. Deborah was outside and there were starlings. It was a beautifully clear evening. We watched the starlings. I love how they come together and move away and then come back together. They sometimes look like half a shape. It's beautiful.

Martha Anthony, can I ask you to do something for me, please?

Anthony Absolutely.

Martha I'm going to time you, I'm going to give you one minute, and in that minute I'd like you to list as many animals as you possibly can beginning with the letter S. Is that clear?

Anthony Okay, alright.

Martha As many animals as you can beginning with the letter S. Ready . . .? Go.

Anthony Ss . . . Ss . . . Sausage dog . . . Hedgehog . . . Ss . . . Shoe . . .

Martha (*beat, then*) Anthony?

Anthony Yes.

Martha Everything alright?

Anthony Everything's fine; are you alright?

Martha I'm very well thank you.

Anthony Would you like me to get you something to drink?

Martha No thank you.

Anthony Have I told you about Deborah?

Martha A little.

Anthony She's extraordinary, really an extraordinary person; do you know about her father?

Martha I don't.

Anthony He died when she was very young.

Martha I'm sorry to hear that.

Anthony He had a heart attack. She told me he used to drink a lot. She read *The Time Machine* and committed to the idea that she could build a time machine and go back to him. She described seeing him in an open casket; he was wearing a blue suit, and she cried and she said 'I'm, I'm sorry. I'm sorry.'

Martha Anthony I wonder –

Anthony Am I talking too much?

Martha No, I want you to talk.

Anthony Do you know what a wormhole is?

Martha I don't. No.

Anthony It's alright, neither did I, why would you? A wormhole used to be called an Einstein–Rosenburg bridge, but it's a tunnel, really, basically. It's a tunnel. It's a tunnel between two parts of the cosmos. If you . . . If you had a bouncy ball and you marked two points on the ball point A and point B on either side of the ball and you drilled a hole you now have two ways to get from A to B. The tunnel in the middle is a wormhole. You could still travel on the surface but you can also use the funnel.

Martha Did you study physics, Anthony?

Anthony Me? No.

Martha What was your subject?

Anthony I'm studying history.

Martha How are you finding it?

Anthony Finding what?

Martha Studying for your degree?

Anthony Have I told you about Deborah?

Martha You know what, Anthony? Let's stop.

Anthony Am I doing alright?

Martha I think we should pick up this conversation another time.

Anthony I love how they come together and move away and then come back together.

Elouise I had a telephone call from Jack Kauffman today.

Harvey Honey –

Elouise You let me finish, you son of a bitch. I had a telephone call from Jack Kauffman, who . . . who wanted to inform me . . .

Harvey Honey –

Elouise How could you, Thomas?

Harvey None of what Jack is –

Elouise Right underneath –

Harvey Jack is spreading a load of baloney –

Elouise You need to leave.

Harvey Honey –

Elouise You need go upstairs and get your things and you need –

Harvey Honey, none of what Jack is saying to you is true. I swear to you. They are – The hospital – They wanna discredit me because o' the brain.

Elouise If I hear one more word about that goddam brain, I swear to God –

Harvey Elouise, honey, listen to me: Jack Kauffman is trying to poison –

Elouise The kids, Thom, what in the hell –

Harvey This whole thing – This whole story – It is a whole heap of baloney –

Elouise Who is she.

Harvey What?

Elouise You heard what I said, you son of a –

Harvey Honey –

Elouise Who is she. (*Beat.*) You tell me who she is right now or –

Harvey Caroline, her name is Caroline Fitzgerald.

Elouise What does she do.

Harvey She's a, she's a nurse. She's one of the assistants.

Elouise She that young girl?

Harvey She is.

Elouise That young girl with the eyebrows?

Harvey I don't know?

Elouise Whaddaya mean, you don't know?

Harvey I mean I don't know, I don't pay attention –

Elouise Oh you wouldn't know about that.

Harvey Honey –

Elouise You wouldn't know about that 'cause you're too damn busy –

Harvey Honey, you need to calm down.

Elouise Don't you –

Harvey Honey, honey, I can see the vein, okay? (*A vein on Elouise's forehead.*) I can see the vein.

Elouise Maybe I wanna burst it, maybe I wanna burst it and maybe I wanna have you clean it up.

Harvey I don't know what that means, okay?

Elouise (*beat*) How long?

Beat.

Elouise How. Long.

Harvey Start of the Fall. Give or take.

Elouise You sleepin' together?

40

Beat.

Elouise Okay. Here's what I need you to do. I need you to leave, right now, and I need you to not come back. I will telephone you at the hospital with a time when the house will be empty and then, and only then, will I allow you back into our home to collect your things. And if you wanna see your children again, you need to stop with this brain.

Harvey I wanna see the boys.

Elouise Do you understand?

Harvey I wanna see the boys, Elouise.

Elouise Then you need to stop with the brain.

Harvey I love you, okay, I swear to you, okay, but listen, the brain, the work with the brain is something that I cannot stop now, you know that. But this thing, this thing with Caroline, it barely even got started, I swear to you. Things at the hospital are tense right now, okay, things are intense and I'm havina deal with a lot of –

Elouise Things're intense.

Harvey Exactly.

Elouise Oh, they're intense, okay, my apologies, I didn't realise –

Harvey There is a lot of opposition to the work I'm tryina do, and I can't talk to you about it because you're so goddam . . .!

Elouise What. So God damn what.

Harvey Every breakthrough is a struggle, okay. And maybe if you supported me, 'steada –

Elouise Supported you, *supported* you, are you kidding me?

41

Harvey Einstein didn't come up with relativity overnight, okay, it took, it took, years, it took *decades*, and at the moment, at this particular moment, the work I'm doing, the research I'm tryina do –

Elouise (*on 'with'*) It's a distraction, it's an obsession, and I'm sicka hearin' about it. It's a pastime –

Elouise Get out.

Harvey Now I cannot tell you what we might be able to uncover, that I cannot tell you. But what I can tell you, is that there is a helluva lot we still don't know. Progress is a destination. 'Chance favours the prepared mind', you know who said that?

Elouise That doesn't mean anything.

Elouise Stop talking.

Elouise Enough. Enough.

Harvey Listen to me, I love you, I swear to God.

Elouise You don't get to say that . . . You do not get to say that . . . You have broken my heart.

Brenda (*groggy*) Richard, what are you doing? It's really late, sweetheart. Trouble sleeping again, what's the matter?

Richard stabs Brenda twice in very quick succession.

Richard!

Richard stabs Brenda nine times in very quick succession.

Storing

Margaret Henry, I have something that I would very much like to ask you.

Henry You sound very serious.

Margaret That's because I have something serious that I want to speak to you about.

Henry Alright.

Beat.

My love . . .?

Margaret I'm all of a sudden very nervous. I might try closing my eyes?

Henry Good idea.

Margaret (*closes eyes; beat*) Here we go. Henry, I love you and I would like for us to become engaged. But I don't know if that is what you want because you are yet to not only ask me but yet to even broach this particular subject in conversation –

Henry Margaret –

Margaret And if the reason you have not yet broached this particular subject in conversation is because you've no desire to –

Henry Margaret –

Margaret But I think it is important that we at least enter into a discussion –

Henry I agree –

Margaret Because we have been in a relationship now –

Henry I know, I'm sorry –

Margaret And if there is a problem regarding –

Henry There is not –

Margaret And as time has gone on, I have struggled with the idea that my role in our engagement is to simply await –

Henry Margaret, I am scared of your father. (*Beat.*) I'm scared of your father.

　　Margaret opens her eyes.

That's why I haven't asked. Because I have been too scared to seek his permission. That is the reason you have not been asked this particular question.

Margaret Scared?

Henry Yes.

Margaret In what way?

Henry Because I find him to be an intimidating man.

Margaret I had no idea.

Henry Good, because I have worked very hard to conceal my fear.

Margaret But why?

　　Henry goes blank. Beat.

Henry?

　　Henry is mentally absent for a few seconds more.

Henry – Henry.

Henry Yes.

Margaret You disappeared.

Henry For how long?

Margaret Only a moment or so.

Henry Oh.

Margaret How do you feel?

Henry I feel ridiculous for having been afraid of your father.

Margaret Don't.

Henry His hands, he has very large hands.

Margaret He's a carpenter.

Henry I worry sometimes that he might . . . I don't know . . . I worry that he already feels you have disadvantaged yourself in light of my seizures –

Margaret I don't care. And he doesn't feel that way.

Henry I also, to speak frankly, I also find his moustache quite intimidating. The hands and the moustache are a particularly intimidating combination.

Margaret I understand. What should we do?

Henry Well. If I may, I think, I think if you were to ask me, then, in my eyes, that would remove the concern I have about the reaction of your father.

Margaret kneels.

But may I, may I ask you a question regarding your father?

Margaret stands.

Henry Does he scare you?

Margaret No.

Henry Not at all?

Margaret No.

Henry Your father does not scare you?

Margaret No.

Henry The hands?

Margaret Henry.

Henry Sorry.

Margaret (*kneels, beat*) Henry Maison, will you marry me?

Henry Yes.

> *Henry has a seizure, a 'grand mal': a stiffening of the limbs followed by rhythmic convulsions.*

Margaret Henry – Henry – Henry!

Henry (*suddenly 'back to normal'*) Hello my love, where have you been?

Margaret Right here. I've been right here.

Henry I thought you'd left?

Margaret No.

Henry Where have you been?

Margaret I've been right here.

Henry I thought you'd left.

Margaret Never.

Martha He was found on the underground without any identification. He says his name's Anthony but we've no way of knowing. At least not yet anyway.

Patricia And, what, he just has no idea who he is?

Martha It's not that he doesn't know who he is but – I don't s'pose you've heard of something called confabulation, have you?

Patricia Is it a dance?

Martha No.

Patricia Is it a board game?

Martha No.

Patricia Then no, I've never heard of it. But it sounds fucking cool whatever it is.

Martha It's not that cool.

Patricia I bet it's gonna be pretty cool.

Martha It's, it's basically a process whereby the brain produces spontaneous, partly made-up, maybe partly not, memories. It's so people with certain disorders or syndromes can continue to function. A damaged brain can continue to make sense of the world even if the patient can't.

Patricia And so, what, he literally can't remember anything?

Martha My instinct would be that he's wiped out his long-term – or rather it's been wiped out. I think. Maybe.

Patricia How come?

Martha Could be substance abuse, might be an injury, a traumatic event – Could be any number of things.

Patricia Fuck. And so, what, he's just sort of stuck, saying and doing and thinking the same things over and over?

Martha It's a bit more complicated than that but, in effect, yes.

Patricia That is fucking tragic.

Martha Interesting.

Patricia What, you don't think so?

Martha I think I probably used to, but, no, I don't feel that way now.

47

Patricia Well, that is the darkest thing I've ever heard in my life. Like, ever.

Martha Or it's liberating – I mean, imagine if you could, if you could forget all the embarrassing things you'd ever done, all the people you loved who are dead and who you desperately miss – Imagine if you could forget all that trauma and all that pain. Having to remember keeps us locked into a particular mode of behaviour – It makes us a certain person. Imagine how liberating it would be to not know who you are. To feel free to behave however you want. To not be sad or self-conscious or afraid of what might be round the corner. Most of the amnesiacs I get to see or work with make a full recovery. More often than not their amnesia is temporary. But for a couple of minutes or a couple of hours, I feel like saying to them: enjoy it while it lasts. I envy the freedom they have to be anyone they want.

Patricia Okay so wait that's different; you're still saying they're in there somewhere, their personality or whatever is still –

Martha No, that's not what I'm saying. If you can't remember who you are then in a way you aren't really anyone.

Patricia Shit the bed, Martha.

Martha I'm sorry?

Patricia What. The. Fuck.

Martha There isn't a, the brain doesn't have some kind of central region that unites all the elements of us. Our brains are constantly, exhaustively working overtime to deliver the illusion that we're in control, but we're not. The brain builds a narrative to steady us from moment to moment, but it's ultimately an illusion. There is no me, there is no you, and there is certainly no self; we are divided and discontinuous and constantly being duped. The brain is a storytelling machine and it's really, really good at fooling us.

Patricia No, you're right, that's not bleak at all.

Martha I know it feels like an appalling revelation, but the moment I stopped seeing my patients as human beings and started seeing them for what they really are – My, my mum, my adoptive mum, she . . . I s'pose what I'm trying to say is, when you, when you, when you look at a brain, say –

Patricia Every other day of the week.

Martha When you really, really look it, you realise, or at least I did: there's nothing. There is nothing there – Nothing *in* there. You can poke it, you can prod it, you can weigh it, you can chop it up –

Patricia Oh my God, did you poke a brain?

Martha What? No.

Patricia I woulda totally fucking poked it.

Martha I didn't poke it.

Patricia How many brains have you seen?

Martha Only a couple.

Patricia You're so blasé. (*A French accent for some reason.*) 'Yeah, sure, I've seen a couple of brains, so what?'

Martha I might need to start thinking about making a move.

Patricia What?

Martha Wanted to try and catch the last tube.

Patricia Stay.

Martha What?

Patricia Stay.

Martha Really?

Patricia You should totally stay. If you want. But I mean if you need to get back –

Martha No – I – That would – Staying sounds . . . I would love that.

Patricia Great. I'll go and make up the spare bedroom. Jokes.

Martha Can I tell you something?

Patricia You definitely can.

Martha I was married.

Patricia (*longish beat*) Okay.

Martha For twenty-one years.

Patricia Okay.

Martha His name is Paul. (*Beat.*) I'm sorry. For not telling you. Sooner. This is all quite new. To me.

Patricia You're divorced, right?

Martha Yes – God – Yes – Absolutely done and dusted.

Patricia Okay.

Martha Patricia, I'm really sorry.

Patricia It's okay. Um, it's a bit . . . odd, but.

Martha If you want to change your mind about me spending the night –

Patricia I might. If that's okay? But not – not for any particularly negative reason – But just because –

Martha I understand.

Patricia Okay.

Beat.

Martha (*perhaps growing a little upset, but not too much*) I really am sorry.

Lisa-Scott Hi, how's it goin', my names's Lisa-Scott; I'm gonna be your waitress.

Harvey Hello Lisa-Scott; I'm Thom.

Lisa-Scott Hi Thom.

Harvey Great accent.

Lisa-Scott Oh yeah, you like my accent?

Harvey What is that, British?

Lisa-Scott I'm from Sydney. Australia.

Harvey Huh.

Lisa-Scott Ever been to Australia, Thom?

Harvey You know, I have not.

Lisa-Scott It's great; you should check it out.

Harvey I will be sure to do that.

Lisa-Scott What about you, where'bouts you from, Thom?

Harvey I'm from Kansas.

Lisa-Scott Local boy.

Harvey You bet. I was in New Jersey. But.

Lisa-Scott What brings you back, Thom?

Harvey Uh, it's kinda complicated, but –

Lisa-Scott Oh, okay.

Harvey I, uh, I kinda went through – I'm kinda recently separated, uh, divorced. I'm kinda recently divorced.

Lisa-Scott I'm sorry to hear that, Thom.

Harvey Thank you, 'preciate that.

Lisa-Scott If it helps, I'm in exactly the same boat.

Harvey What? No. You gotta be . . . kidding me, right?

Lisa-Scott 'Fraid not, Thom.

Harvey You mind if I ask your age?

Lisa-Scott Top secret information I'm afraid, Thom.

Harvey No, I get that. That was rude.

Lisa-Scott I'm yanking ya chain, Thom, relax.

Harvey Got it.

Lisa-Scott So what can I get for you, Thom?

Harvey Lisa-Scott, I would love a short stack o' pancakes with a side o' bacon.

Lisa-Scott Bad news I'm afraid, Thom; we finished servin' breakfast 'bout an hour ago.

Harvey You make an exception for a local boy?

Lisa-Scott 'Fraid not.

Harvey What time is it?

Lisa-Scott It's a quarter after three.

Harvey What?

Lisa-Scott A quarter after three.

Harvey My watch has stopped.

Lisa-Scott Guess that explains it.

Harvey Dammit.

Lisa-Scott Interest you in a cheeseburger, Thom?

Harvey Sure, maybe.

Lisa-Scott Whaddaya say?

Harvey Sure.

Lisa-Scott You want fries?

Harvey You bet.

Lisa-Scott Any sides with that?

Harvey Kinda sides you got?

Lisa-Scott We got every kinda side.

Harvey Oh yeah?

Lisa-Scott Coleslaw, potato salad, whipped potatoes, baked potato, homemade potato chips, cottage fries, fried okra, fried cornmeal mush, fried apples, apple sauce, soup o' the day, fried cheese sticks, onion rings . . . you name it.

Harvey Wow. Well. May I please have a side of cottage fries . . . and a side of fried cornmeal mush?

Lisa-Scott Coming right up.

Harvey Actually, sorry, you know what? I might see if I can find somewhere else open that's still serving pancakes.

Lisa-Scott Thom, ya breaking my heart right now.

Harvey I didn't mean to cause any offence –

Lisa-Scott Tell you what? You wait around maybe an hour or so, and I'll be done.

Harvey Oh, okay.

Lisa-Scott And if you wanna come back to my place, I'll make you a short stack myself.

Harvey Is this – Are you – Is my chain being – Earlier on –

Lisa-Scott No yanking involved whatsoever this time. Cross my heart.

Harvey Okay, well, wow. Sold.

Margaret Hello Henry.

Henry Hello my love.

Margaret Hello.

Henry It's good to see you.

Margaret You too.

Henry I've been feeling a bit under the weather.

Margaret In what way?

Henry I'm not sure, tell you the truth.

Margaret How have you been sleeping?

Henry Not too bad.

Margaret What about last night?

Henry Tell you the truth, I didn't stay awake to find out.

Margaret (*smiles, then*) Henry?

Henry Yes, my love.

Margaret I need you to really listen to me. I . . . I have to go away for a day or two. Perhaps longer.

Henry Can I come with you?

Margaret Not this time.

Henry That's a shame.

Margaret It won't be very long.

Henry I understand.

Margaret I'm going to leave you with a book of crossword puzzles.

Henry That's very kind of you.

Margaret When I see you again, you can read me the answers.

Henry Are you sure you don't need me to come with you?

Margaret I'm sure. (*Beat.*) Henry?

Henry Hello my love.

Margaret Hello Henry.

Henry Where have you been?

Margaret Henry, I need you to really listen to me. I have to go away. For a day or two. Perhaps longer.

Henry Can I come with you?

Margaret Not this time

Henry That's a shame.

Margaret I'm going to leave you with a book of crossword puzzles.

Henry That's very kind of you.

Margaret When I see you again, you can read me the answers.

Henry Are you sure you don't need me to come with you?

Margaret I'm sure. (*Beat.*) Henry?

Henry Yes, my love.

Margaret I love you.

Henry I know.

Margaret Good. (*Kisses Henry, then:*) Goodbye, Henry.

Martha (*a little drunk*) Her name's Patricia.

Ben How'd you meet?

Martha You're not allowed to laugh at me. *Guardian* Soulmates.

Ben That's great.

Martha You're not gonna call me a loser?

Ben I'm not gonna call you a loser, no, because it's not the eighties and people don't use that word any more.

Martha Don't be ironic. It isn't clever or interesting.

Ben Nor is turning up drunk at –

Martha I am not drunk.

Ben Aren't you?

Martha I am not drunk.

Ben Fine. What d'you want?

Martha I thought we ought to catch up.

Ben What?

Martha How are you, Ben? Thank you for the CD; I enjoyed it very much.

Ben I'm gonna be doing a couple of gigs, actually

Martha When?

Ben Couple of weeks' time.

Martha Why didn't you tell me?

Ben I only just found out.

Martha You need to keep me better informed.

Ben Mum, I only just found out.

Martha Where?

Ben Borderline, Union Chapel, couple of others.

Martha I don't know those places but I feel confident that both they and you will be brilliant.

Ben Thanks.

Martha Will you email me the dates?

Ben I will.

Martha How's Claire?

Ben She's good.

Martha Good, is that all I get?

Ben Mum, what're you doing here?

Martha What?

Ben What d'you want? It's late.

Martha Tough.

Ben What?

Martha Tough shit. How – Do you have any idea how many times – Well, you know what, it's about time we turn the tables, my friend –

Ben I have no idea what you're talking about.

Martha When you used to pitch up at the house, middle of the morning, wailing about some girl or some something-or-other, I never – Can you imagine –

Ben I was –

Martha 'Magine if I'd turned you away –

Ben I was a –

Martha I don't know what I'm doing. I'm sorry.

Ben What does she do?

Martha Who?

Ben I've forgotten her name already, sorry?

Martha Patricia. Solicitor. Was.

Ben How many dates've you been on?

Martha Two. Three.

Ben You really like her?

  Martha nods.

(*Beat.*) Do you want something to eat?

Martha What've you got?

Ben What d'you fancy?

Martha Have you got any Nutella?

Ben No.

Martha Call yourself a host . . .

Ben Does she know about me?

Martha No. The straight marriage was enough of a bombshell.

  Ben laughs a little.

Do you wish I hadn't left your father?

Ben Mum.

Martha What?

Ben Don't ask me things like that.

Martha Sorry.

Ben I saw Dad last week.

Martha And?

Ben D'you really wanna know?

Martha Was he good or bad?

Ben He was good.

Martha Then, no, I don't want to know.

Ben Got it.

Martha Fuck him.

Ben Understood.

Martha Did I fuck up our family?

Ben No.

Martha Okay. Can I go to sleep now?

Freddy (*stoned*) Oh my God, you're the guy?

Lisa-Scott (*stoned*) He's the guy.

Anna (*stoned*) No way?

Freddy You're *the* guy?

Harvey I am.

Freddy Fuckin' A, man, fuckin' A.

Anna My mom was obsessed with that story.

Lisa-Scott Right?

Freddy You totally took that guy's brain, man. Fuckin' stole it.

Harvey I didn't steal it.

Freddy Fuckin' brain thief.

Harvey I didn't steal it.

Anna (*laughs*) He didn't steal it . . . !

Freddy Oh my God, I don't even know where to begin with this guy . . .

Harvey I obtained the brain entirely legitimately.

Anna How'd you do it?

Harvey I'm a pathologist.

Lisa-Scott Thom, you sure you don't wanna smoke some pot?

Harvey No thank you.

Freddy I wanna fuckin' salute you, man. Fuckin' royalty right here!

Lisa-Scott Tell 'em how you did it.

Anna How'd he die?

Freddy This shit is so fucked up.

Harvey How did the professor die?

Anna Yes.

Harvey Internal bleeding.

Anna That is so sad.

Freddy (*reflective*) Internal bleeding, God damn.

Lisa-Scott Tell 'em 'bout the brain.

Freddy Hold up: you mean you still got it?

Harvey Sure.

Anna You still got the brain?

Harvey Sure.

Lisa-Scott He keeps it in these little jars?

Freddy I swear to God, if you're lyin' to me –

Lisa-Scott Tell 'em.

Harvey I . . . still have the brain, yes.

Freddy Sir, you are a god damn legend.

Anna What's it look like?

Harvey Well. Kinda like a brain.

Freddy I knew it.

Anna Do brains rot?

Harvey Excuse me?

Anna Does it rot, you know, decompose?

Harvey Well, it's preserved.

Anna Oh yeah?

Harvey Sure.

Freddy 'Preserved'.

Harvey You gotta . . . I used a paraformaldehyde solution.

Freddy Exactly.

Harvey You have to work quickly. By submerging the brain in the formaldehyde, you capture it, you freeze it, midstream. You capture the brain cells almost as if in mid-thought, so that when it comes to slicing the brain up, what you're lookin' at is as close to a living brain as –

Anna You sliced it up?

Harvey Sure.

Anna You actually sliced up the brain?

Freddy Salami, man, I'm tellin' you.

Harvey Well, it's not quite salami, but I, uh, I take your point.

Anna Then what? Once you sliced it up.

Harvey We sealed each of the slices in a mixture of paraffin and water . . . then we, uh, we photographed the various, uh, slices.

Freddy I gotta shake your hand.

Anna Can we see it?

Harvey Way-ell . . .

Lisa-Scott He's pretty protective. I haven't even seen it.

Anna What're you, I mean whattayou even gonna do with it?

Harvey Well. We're gonna study it. We are studying it.

Freddy Exactly.

Harvey And let me tell you, it has not been easy. You know when Einstein first submitted the, uh, his Special Theory of Relativity as his doctoral thesis, it was rejected. There was a lot of animosity around that whole area.

Freddy God damn it.

Harvey But you know he worked at it, and he worked at it, and he changed our understanding of the entire universe. But it did not happen overnight.

Freddy Amen to that.

Anna But what're you actually doing?

Freddy Exactly.

Harvey Excuse me?

Anna You, you, what are you actually doing?

Freddy Exactly.

Harvey Well. I'm in charge. I'm in charge of the research.

Anna But I mean, who gives a shit?

Freddy Exactly my point.

Harvey I'm not sure I understand the question?

Lisa-Scott Leave him alone. Ignore 'em, Thom.

Harvey I don't mind.

Anna Science, fuckin' science, I mean enough already, right?

Freddy Kansas has more rainbows than any other US state. Fact. Science.

Harvey Would you like me to respond to your –

Anna Sure. Go right ahead.

Harvey But are you actually going to listen to me?

Anna I am all of my ears.

Freddy 'Ears'.

Harvey A hundred years ago, okay –

Anna I'm listening.

Harvey A hundred years ago we thought the universe was static. We had no idea of its scale, its extraordinary scope. We used to believe that our galaxy was the only galaxy. And then all of a sudden we realised we were simply one of hundreds, thousands, just hanging there. We went from being the centre of the universe to just some little piece. But it sure as hell didn't happen overnight. Science confounds and enlightens through its continued and systematic observation of our world, exactly as it is.

Freddy Exactly.

Harvey I believe the next great endeavour is the mapping of the brain. Exactly as we have mapped the cosmos, we now need to map out the human brain. Because if you can understand the ingredients, the components, that make us who we are, then my God you can understand everything. And there is no bit of the brain that can't be studied, or weighed, or measured, or cut open; there isn't a gland or a ventricle inaccessible to the surgeon's knife. And what better place to start, what better place to begin, than by examining the brain of one of the greatest scientific minds of the twentieth century. 'Chance favours the prepared mind', you know who said that?

> *Beat. Then Anna bursts out laughing.*
> *Freddy bursts out laughing.*

Why are they laughing?

Anna Oh my God, where did you find this guy?

Harvey I don't understand?

Lisa-Scott Guys, come on.

Freddy 'Chance favours the prepared mind'!

Lisa-Scott Leave him alone.

Anna Where did you find this guy?

Freddy Man, you are some kinda freak. Mean I like you, but you are like . . . (*Beginning to calm down, beginning to stop laughing.*) I gotta eat.

Anna Yes.

Freddy Doc, you hungry?

> *Harvey doesn't respond.*

Lisa-Scott I think he's ignoring you.

Freddy What'd we do?

Harvey I would like to leave now.

Freddy Hey, Doc, come on, siddown.

Harvey Don't you tell me what to do, you little, you little *prick*.

Anna Whoa –

Freddy Hey –

Anna That is uncalled for.

Freddy Like, so uncalled for.

Anna Like, oh my God so uncalled for.

Harvey (*crestfallen*) This is my . . . life, it is my . . .

Lisa-Scott (*beat*) Guys, I think we're gonna shoot.

Victor Henry, we have already spoken about this. Margaret won't be coming to see you again. I'm sorry.

Henry Does she know where I am?

Victor It's . . . It's all rather complicated, I'm afraid, Henry.

Henry She will only worry if we don't tell her where I am, you see.

Victor I understand, but –

Henry I hope you're not misinforming me?

Victor Most certainly not. Henry, I don't wish to speak to you about Margaret again, I wish to speak to you about something else entirely. I'm . . . Concerns have recently been raised about my health and, as such –

Henry I'm very sorry to hear that.

Victor Yes. As such –

Henry Is there anything I can do?

Victor Henry, will you listen to me for goodness sake! I need to stop working, for a short while. You will be left in very good hands, I've no doubt. Indeed, I will make sure of it. Do you understand? Henry?

Henry . . .

Victor Henry?

Henry Hello.

Victor Hello Henry.

Henry I'm sorry I don't think we've met?

Victor . . .

Henry You're not related to Janet Fletcher are you?

Victor I'm afraid I'm not.

Henry I wonder if you might be able to help me find my wife? Margaret?

Victor Henry, my name is Dr Milner. Dr Victor Milner. I –

Henry Doctor . . . ?

Victor Milner. Dr Victor Milner.

Henry I wonder if you might have your wires crossed?

Victor Henry: Margaret won't be coming to see you.

Henry We're supposed to travelling to London?

Victor Margaret . . . Margaret isn't coming to see you, Henry. Nor – Indeed nor can I. I am hopeful my absence will be temporary. But I am sorry that I cannot say the same for Margaret.

Henry I'm a bit confused?

Victor You will be extremely well looked after, Henry, do you understand? That much I can promise you.

Henry . . .

Victor Henry . . . ?

Henry Hello.

Victor Hello Henry.

Henry I'm sorry I don't think we've met?

Victor As a matter of fact, we have.

Henry Oh. My apologies.

Victor You mustn't apologise. Take care of yourself, Henry.

Patricia Hi.

Martha Hi.

Patricia (*beat*) How's it going?

Martha Good. Thanks. You?

Patricia Okay.

Martha Do you want to come inside?

Patricia No thanks. Haven't got long. Meeting some friends. Nearby. So thought I'd.

Martha Where are you meeting them?

Patricia That was a lie. I was tryina play it cool. Which, clearly . . .

Martha Why don't you come in?

Patricia I have two things to say. The first one is unrelated to us and the second is entirely about us.

Martha Why don't you start with the first thing?

Patricia A guy I went to law school with is looking for an expert witness and I was talking to him about you and – Anyway you can prob'ly guess where this is going: I was wondering if I could put you two in touch?

Martha Of course.

Patricia Great.

Martha Email is probably best.

Patricia The second thing is obviously about the fact that you used to be married and that, upon learning this, I perhaps flipped out and lost my shit a little unnecessarily.

Martha You didn't –

Patricia I sort of did and I sort of didn't; it's a moot point. But the bit that's un-moot, or whatever the opposite of moot is – What is the opposite of moot?

Martha I don't know.

Patricia Point being I'm sorry if I overreacted.

Martha You'd –

Patricia But what I don't get, sorry, is why you didn't just put 'divorced' on your profile? If you'd done that, I probably wouldn't have been that bothered, but the fact that you didn't and you held off telling me –

Martha I didn't tell you –

Patricia I'm just saying as long as there's nothing else like major that I ought to know about then, you know, I would like to come back and see you another time when I'm not pretending I'm meeting friends.

Beat. Patricia moves to Martha and kisses her; soft, tender. Beat.

Patricia You alright?

Martha Yeah, no. I'm fine.

Otto Dear Dr Harvey, You may be surprised hearing from me after such a long time during which there has been no correspondences. A friend sent me recently an article which was published in the *Kansas City Times* under the title 'Einstein's Brain Still a Convoluted Puzzle'. I am writing you to renew our acquaintance of almost thirty years, but also to enquire about your present intention to describe and publish your work on Einstein's brain. I believe we owe the scientific world and also laymen some – positive or negative – results of the research on Einstein's brain. I hope that all has been well with your family and yourself and wish you would be kind enough to remember me to your wife whose acquaintance I was so happy to make when you were living in New Jersey. With kind regards, Otto Nathan, Executor and Trustee.

Retrieving

Michael Morning.

Harvey Good morning.

Michael My name's Michael. I just moved in to number forty-three.

Harvey Way-ell, welcome to the neighbourhood, Michael.

Michael Thank you; 'preciate that.

Harvey Good to have you.

Michael And sorry, your name is . . . ?

Harvey Thom. Thom Harvey.

Michael Good to meet you, Thom.

Harvey Settlin' in okay?

Michael Yes, sir. So far.

Harvey You take care now.

Michael Sorry, Thom?

Harvey Yessir.

Michael It's not . . . Dr Harvey, is it, Dr Thomas Harvey?

Harvey . . .

Michael Pathologist Dr Thomas Harvey?

Harvey Can I help you with something?

Michael Okay, full disclosure: my wife and I are science nuts and we would love to take you out for dinner some time.

Harvey That right.

Michael You like sushi?

Harvey Sushi?

Michael Raw fish. It's a –

Harvey I, uh, I know what kinda food sushi is.

Michael We know a great place.

Harvey You lemme think about it?

Michael Absolutely.

Harvey Good meetin' you, Michael.

Michael You'll let me know.

Harvey You bet.

Michael Pleasure meeting you, sir.

Jon Hello Henry, how are you this morning?

Henry I can't seem to find my cigarettes.

Jon I thought you'd given up?

Henry Oh.

Jon You're not allowed to smoke in here, anyway.

Henry I was almost certain . . .

Jon How did you sleep, Henry?

Henry Tell you the truth, I didn't stay awake to find out.

Jon Henry, do you know who I am?

Henry You're not related to Janet Fletcher are you?

Jon I am definitely not related to Janet Fletcher, no. But what if I told you my first name was Jon . . . ?

Henry Um . . .

Jon Take your time.

Henry Williams . . . ?

Jon (*genuinely excited*) Henry, you clever bugger, well done. And what do you think it is that I do, Henry? What's my job?

Henry Surgeon . . . ?

Jon Ooh, not quite, but you're very close. I'm a doctor; a professor, Henry.

Henry I'm sorry if I get a little mixed up.

Jon It's not a problem.

Henry I have trouble remembering things, you see.

Jon Henry, I wondered if I might be able to ask you a couple of questions?

Henry Certainly.

Jon Some of these questions might seem a bit bizarre, but bear with me, alright?

Henry I will do my best.

Jon I'd like you to count to twenty please, Henry.

Henry Certainly. One, two, three, four, five, six, seven, eight, nine, ten, eleven . . . eleven . . .

Jon (*beat*) Henry?

Henry I'm sorry?

Jon Hello Henry, I'm Jon.

Henry Hello Jon.

Jon Henry, I was wondering if I might be able to ask you some questions?

Henry I wonder if you might be able to help me find my wife? Her name is Margaret.

Jon Henry –

Henry I'm starting to worry about her . . .

Jon Henry, I'm going to read you a series of numbers, out loud, and what I'd like you to do, Henry, is to repeat each one in turn back to me, alright?

Henry Yes.

Jon Alright, here we go. Four six nine.

Henry Four six nine.

Jon Eight two six five.

Henry Eight two six five.

Jon Brilliant. Here's the next one: ten three five seven two.

Henry Ten three five seven two.

Jon Yes, Henry. Okay. Nine seven three ten one six.

Henry Nine . . .

Jon Would you like me to give you the number one more time?

Henry I think so.

Jon Nine seven three ten one six.

Henry Nine seven three ten one . . . six.

Jon Henry: really well done. How do we feel about one more?

Henry . . .

Jon Henry?

Henry I'm trying to think!

Jon Alright, fair enough.

    Beat.

Henry, is everything alright?

    Henry shakes his head, growing upset.

Jon Alright, I think we should call it a day. Henry: you've done brilliantly. Alright? Bloody brilliantly.

Henry I'm worried about Margaret . . .

Martha Greg?

Greg Yes. Martha?

Martha I'm so sorry I'm late.

Greg Don't worry about it.

Martha I had a call from my son just as I was about to leave.

Greg Nice coat.

Martha Thank you.

Greg Looks great on you.

Martha Thank you.

Greg Think you've got something in your –

    He picks something from Martha's hair.

Martha Oh.

Greg Fly or summin'.

Martha Odd.

Greg What conditioner d'you use?

Martha Sorry?

Greg Conditioner.

Martha John Frieda?

Greg Nice. Listen I hope you don't mind standing?

Martha It was like this last time I was here.

Greg You've been here before?

Martha With Patricia, Pat, yes.

Greg Great place, right?

Martha Mmm.

Greg So thanks for meeting with me, Martha. Pat speaks very highly of you.

Martha How do you know Patricia?

Greg We were at law school together.

Martha Yes.

Greg Back in the day.

Martha Right.

Greg Pat's so great.

Martha She is.

Greg We used to go out. Put that out there.

Martha Oh, okay.

Greg Those were fuckin' wild days.

Martha Really.

Greg I fuckin' love Pat. Mean she fuckin', she was fuckin'. Up for it. D'you know what I mean? And I mean not in a slutty way or anything.

Martha No.

Greg Not in a slutty way At All. Mean that's what I like about the whole bisexual movement. Mean I'm straight, don't get me wrong. But. Honestly some of the nicest people I've spent time with often swing both ways.

Martha Interesting.

Greg So look, Martha, obviously I don't need to tell you that anything you and I discuss this afternoon is –

Martha No, of course, I understand.

Greg It's a juicy case, Martha, I'll tell you that much. Married couple, mid-fifties, husband is on anti-depressants, has been for the best part of twenty years. It's their thirtieth anniversary so they decide to go away. Only problem is, y'man's medication has one particularly unfortunate side effect. Kills his libido, dead. Dick's as limp as roadkill. Has been for best part of ten years. So he comes off.

Martha Comes off the anti-depressants?

Greg Comes off the anti-depressants so him and his wife can have a right good session, if y'see what I'm saying?

Martha Loud and clear.

Greg So off they go. They drive for I don't even know what, four hundred miles, 'cross the country, and they stay in some remote bit of Scotland. At this point, y'man's been off his medication for approximately a week.

Martha A week?

Greg A week. And as far as we know, so far no issues. After two days, he starts having trouble sleeping. On the third night, he wakes up, early hours of the morning, and stabs his wife of exactly thirty years eleven times. Next morning, he wakes up and he's fucking horrified; devastated. Calls the police and says his wife's been attacked.

Martha Jesus.

Greg He's been on remand for six months since the arrest. Crucially, he has no memory whatsoever of the attack.

Martha Wow.

Greg So bringing it up to date, we're looking to plead automatism and we're after an expert witness to help us with an MRI, EEG and a full written assessment. So look –

Martha I'm . . . I'm sorry but I don't think I'm the right person for the job.

Greg Oh no?

Martha No, I'm sorry.

Greg From what Pat tells me –

Martha I – I suppose the problem is I disagree with the basic –

Greg Sorry, I didn't quite catch that?

Martha I'm not sure that I could say with any great confidence that this man was any more or less in control of his actions than he ordinarily –

Greg Let's track this back for a moment.

Martha If I could finish –

Greg Course.

Martha I don't – I don't necessarily agree with the legal view of responsibility.

Greg Get you.

Martha I'm sorry?

Greg I'm windin' you up.

Martha Why would you do that?

Greg Do what?

Martha I thought we were having a serious conversation.

Greg We are.

Martha Then why are you making jokes?

Greg Okay. Wow. Sorry, okay; my bad. Why don't we talk about fee?

Martha I'm not interested in money –

Greg You're not?

Martha I don't want money.

Greg D'you not believe in money either?

Martha I'm – I'm sorry; I don't know what Patricia told you –

Greg Martha: calm it down. Just hear me out. That's all I'm asking.

Martha I understand that, but I don't want to waste your time, that's all.

Greg Maybe we should head somewhere else?

Martha What?

Greg I know a great Mexican place literally hundred yards away.

Martha I don't want to eat Mexican food with you.

Greg Why not?

Martha Because I don't want to.

Greg It's on the firm.

Martha I'm not hungry.

Greg Coffee then.

Martha I find you strange and I don't like the way you talk about Patricia.

Greg What?

Martha You're strange, you're weird – You touched my hair when I arrived which was a strange thing to do –

Greg Martha, mate.

He takes a hold of Martha.

Martha Please don't touch me.

Greg Martha – Martha – Seriously –

Martha If you touch me again I'll break your fingers. I'm serious, I'll break your fingers and then I'll walk off, I'll walk off and no one will know it was me who did it.

Greg Mate, fuck's sake, calm it down.

Martha No, you calm it down. Goodbye, Greg. I hope we never see each other again.

Greg Jesus, what a cunt.

Harvey Come again?

Michael A road trip.

Harvey Okay.

Michael You and me. You and me, we go see Evelyn, and we show her the brain.

Harvey Evelyn Einstein?

Michael Evelyn Einstein.

Harvey You wanna show –

Michael I wanna show Evelyn Einstein the brain. I called her, Doc. I called her up and I told her 'bout you, 'bout the conversations you and I had been having, and she said, 'Okay: tell me more.' So I did, I said, I said, I said, 'Look: it's all bullshit. All of it. You wanna know the truth? Thomas Harvey is a decent guy. Now how do I know that? Because I met the guy and we ate sushi together, that's how I know.'

Harvey Michael –

Michael I wanna write about the whole history. Not some shitty, tell-all bullshit piece o' junk; we're talking reportage, Doc.

Harvey You curse too much.

Michael I wanna write about family, about heritage; about science.

Harvey You wanna innerview me?

Michael In part, sure. I wan' us to spend some time together. I wanna get to know you, Doc.

Harvey What you see is what you get, Michael.

Michael Bullshit.

Harvey We oughta get you some soap.

Michael Listen. I know you don't like talkin' about it, and I respect that. I do. But, okay, look, here's the thing: next year is gonna be the fortieth anniversary of the professor's death.

Harvey (*beat*) Huh.

Michael Y'see what I'm sayin'? It's a great time, Doc.

Harvey You spoke to Evelyn?

Michael You better believe it.

Harvey Called her up?

Michael Called her up.

Harvey She still livin' in Albany?

Michael Berkeley.

Harvey Berkeley?

Michael Exactly.

Harvey Hell of a distance.

Michael Exactly.

Harvey Lotta gas.

Michael Well –

Harvey That's some expenditure.

Michael The magazine'll cover it.

Harvey The magazine . . .?

Michael Sure. I gotta run it past my editor, but sure.

Harvey Huh.

Michael Y'see what I'm saying? *Harper's*, Doc; we're talking quality.

Harvey Huh.

Michael Listen, take some time to think about it.

Jon Henry, I'd like to introduce you to someone. This is Sharon.

Henry I'm not . . .

Sharon Hello Henry.

Jon Henry –

Henry I'm sick of having this argument with myself.

Jon Henry, Sharon works at Queen's Square. In London.

Sharon I'm a brain donation nurse.

Henry I am sick and tired of having this same argument over and over –

Jon Okay, Henry –

Henry I am asking you to stay out of my way.

Jon Understood.

> *Jon moves himself and Sharon out of Henry's eyeline.*
> *Jon and Sharon deliberately wait . . . and then*
> *re-engage with Henry.*

Hello Henry. Henry, I'd like to introduce you to someone.

Sharon Hello Henry, I'm Sharon.

Henry We haven't met before, have we?

Sharon No.

Henry I have trouble remembering things you see.

Sharon I know. It's why I wanted to come and speak to you.

Jon You're famous, Henry.

Henry I'm . . .

Sharon Neurological royalty.

Henry No, I'm . . .

Sharon You're a very important person, Henry.

Jon VIP.

Henry I'm no good to anyone.

Jon Don't be ridiculous; we'd all be out of a job if it weren't for you.

Sharon Which is why I wanted to come and talk to you about tissue donation. Do you –

Henry No, I'm no good to . . . I'm in the way. I'm in the way. I'm in the way.

Jon Okay –

Henry suddenly shoves Jon, a burst of raw aggression; Jon is understandably taken aback.

Henry Where is she? WHERE IS SHE? You're lying to me –

Jon Nobody is –

Henry You are lying to me, you are, you are lying, and you are –

Jon Henry, I need you to try and –

Henry again shoves Jon.

Henry Stay out of my way.

Jon Understood.

Henry Stay out of my way.

Jon raises his hands; a peaceful gesture.
Henry is very upset all of a sudden. The following might not be entirely audible.

I'm going to kill myself I'm going to kill myself if I, if I . . .

Jon . . .

Henry (*to Sharon*) Margaret.

Jon Henry, this is Sharon.

Sharon Hello Henry.

Henry Hello my love . . .

Jon No, Henry, this is Sharon.

Martha Anthony?

Anthony We met at a party. That's the good thing about the first year of undergraduate study, you get to interact with students from other subjects. I went outside to have a cigarette. I asked her what her subject was and she said physics. She was quite drunk, we both were.

Martha Anything else?

Anthony I remember she told me her father had died when she was very young. He had a heart attack. She told me he used to read to her from *The Time Machine*. She said to me that she was obsessed with that book and that that was what drew her to physics. She committed to the idea that she could build a time machine and go back to him. And she loved Albert Einstein.

Martha Did she?

Anthony Oh yeah. She fell in love with him because of how he changed our understanding of time. Deborah told me that before Einstein, time seemed like a river, flowing in one direction; yesterday the past is upstream and we can never get back to it, and tomorrow is downstream and we're constantly being swept along by the tide. But Einstein said no, it isn't like that.

Martha Anything else?

Anthony I can remember our first night together.

Martha You do?

Anthony Oh yeah. I was sick. I'd had too much to drink. I threw up all over her bathroom. I blocked the sink. It was so embarrassing.

Martha What did Deborah say?

Anthony She . . . Do you know, I'm not quite sure.

Martha Don't worry.

Anthony She made a pot of coffee, I remember that. The morning after. We ended up talking about Einstein. He died when he was seventy-six. I can't remember what it was that killed him, but it had the most extraordinary name. She told me that the person who did the . . . I'm not sure what you call it? You examine the, to try and work out what the problems were . . .

Martha Don't worry.

Anthony The bloke who did the thing on Einstein took his brain. And his eyes. And Einstein was cremated. He was cremated without his brain and without his eyes. Awful. The bloke was a lunatic; he threw himself off the Brooklyn Bridge. We're only aware of a tiny amount of what's happening was what she said.

Martha What do you mean?

Anthony . . .

Martha Anthony? Anthony.

Anthony Yes.

Martha Alright?

Anthony I think so.

85

Martha Anthony, I don't know if I can help you, do you understand? You're not going to see Deborah again. And I, I don't know what to do with you. (*Beat.*) Maybe we ought to stop . . .

Anthony Margaret, can I ask you a question?

Martha Martha.

Anthony What?

Martha My name is Martha.

Anthony What did I say?

Martha Margaret.

Anthony Have I told you about Deborah?

Martha You have.

Anthony Is she on her way, do you think?

Martha No.

Anthony I'm starting to get a bit worried about her.

Martha I know.

Anthony Imagination is more important than knowledge. Knowledge is limited. Imagination encircles the world – do you know who said that?

Martha Who?

Harvey It's a real honour to make your acquaintance.

Evelyn Evelyn; it's a pleasure. Get you fellas something to drink?

Harvey } No thank you.
Michael } Oh, no thank you.

Evelyn Then let's talk . . . brains.

Harvey You bet.

Evelyn You performed the whole autopsy single-handedly,
Dr Harvey, correct?

Harvey You bet.

Evelyn All of it?

Harvey Yes ma'am.

Evelyn What was that like?

Harvey Humbling.

Evelyn You weigh the brain?

Harvey You bet.

Evelyn How much'd it weigh?

Harvey Just over two and half pounds.

Evelyn That it?

Harvey That's a pretty normal weight for a brain.

Evelyn Oh yeah?

Harvey You bet.

Evelyn May I see it?

Harvey Absolutely.

*Michael passes Harvey a small, brown cardboard box.
Harvey removes from the box a smallish bell jar, filled
with liquid, and home to several pieces of Albert
Einstein's brain. Harvey passes the bell jar to Evelyn.*

Careful now.

*Evelyn takes the bell jar and, gazing at it, inspects its
contents.*

Those are, I believe, from the professor's hippocampus.
We attribute short- and long-term memory to this
particular region of the brain.

Beat.

Ma'am?

Evelyn Dr Harvey, may I share something with you?

Harvey Please. And call me Thom.

Evelyn Well, Thom, it was . . . put to me, recently, that I
had not been told the entire truth about my lineage. It
was put to me, that the man I thought to be my adopted
father, Hans Albert, was in fact my brother, and that
Albie might in fact be my father. It appears that when
Albie was sixty-two, he had an affair with a ballet dancer.
The New York Ballet. Albie's executor, a gentleman
named Otto Nathan, kept Albie's, kept my father's,
indiscretion well and truly buried right up until the day
he passed away. Dr Harvey, I wonder if you might be
kind enough to bring your research to a close? I wonder
if you would be so kind as to return the brain. To me. In
its entirety.

Harvey I, uh . . . I'm sorry, I'm, I'm not quite sure I . . .

Evelyn My hope is that the brain can be used to perform
a DNA test. I wish to understand who I am..

Harvey I can . . . I can certainly give you a portion of
the . . . But I'm, I'm sorry, there is still a great deal of
work that *needs* to be done.

Evelyn How so?

Harvey Studies, there are still . . . We have, we have
portions of . . . all over the world. Some of the, some of
the top guys in . . . We have guys in, in Tokyo, Germany,
Canada –

Evelyn Dr Harvey –

Harvey And, and, and recently, I've been working with a gentleman named Britt Abraham from the University of Alabama and, and Britt and I, we, we have a paper coming out. We have a paper coming out. Alterations in cortical thickness and neuronal density in the frontal cortex of –

Evelyn ⎱ Thom, if I may –

Michael ⎰ Doc –

Harvey And, and, and Steven Pinker, you know Steven Pinker? He's going to be –

Evelyn Dr Harvey –

Harvey In the *New York Times*, he's going to be writing about –

Evelyn Thom, I think you and I both know that there is nothing whatsoever remarkable about Albie's brain.

Harvey No.

Evelyn Albie worked like a dog and he treated his family like crap.

Harvey No.

Evelyn He worked and he worked and he worked day after day after day and he found the time and the energy required to do so through sheer neglect. Most of my family, Dr Harvey, they hated Albie. They loathed him. They found him to be arrogant, selfish –

Harvey No. Your grandfather –

Evelyn Albie was not a genius because of his brain; he was a genius because he worked himself to death.

Harvey A hundred years ago we thought the universe was static. We had no idea of its scale, its extraordinary scope. But he changed all that, your –

Michael Doc –

Harvey No, we, we went from being the centre of the universe to just some little piece. But it sure as hell didn't happen overnight. Science proceeds and confounds and enlightens through its continued and systematic observation of our world, exactly as it is.

Evelyn Doc: enough.

Harvey 'Chance favours the prepared mind', you know who said that?

Evelyn It's time to stop, Thom.

Harvey I'm . . . I'm sorry, but I, I cannot do that.

Evelyn Don't apologise.

Harvey I cannot share your point of view. I wanna help you, Evelyn, but stopping is something that I cannot . . . I'm sorry.

Evelyn I understand.

Jon Martha?

Martha Yes.

Jon Jon.

Martha Jon, hi.

Jon Thank you for meeting with me; I know you must be very busy.

Martha Occasionally.

Jon Occasionally; I like that. So . . . I have absolutely no idea where to begin. So I'll start at the start and you just tell me if you want me to hurry the hell up and get to the end. Now, and this is going back, God, donkey's years, I was given the opportunity to meet a patient named HM.

Martha Wow.

Jon I know; turned out this bloke I'd read about during my PhD was in a home half an hour down the road. Since that first meeting, I've met with Henry, on and off, once or twice a month across virtually the whole of my career. Some months I see more of Henry than I do my own wife. Henry recently turned eighty and, as such, one thing I am very personally keen to do is ensure that we are given the opportunity to study Henry's brain following his death.

Martha Of course.

Jon In order to secure a donation, we've had to explore various, how do I put this, 'avenues'. One of which, of course, was whether or not Henry has any living relatives. Now I have to be honest with you, Martha, I have agonised over the appropriate – Let alone – Anyway, the best thing might be to just . . .

Jon hands Martha a sheet or two of paper. Beat.

Henry was married to a lady named Margaret who very sadly died giving birth to their first, well, only I suppose, daughter. Henry's pre- and post-operative consultant, a bloke named Victor Milner, made various attempts, according to his notes this is, to break the bad news to Henry. But of course Henry's condition meant that he couldn't even remember to forget. He asks for her even now.

Martha Jesus.

Jon Henry and Margaret's daughter was adopted and, in 1971, at the age of eighteen, she gave birth herself and . . . well, you can, you can read the rest for yourself I'm sure.

Martha (*beat*) Can I hang on to this?

Jon My God – please. I thought for the sake of clarity I'd try and condense everything into a single document.

Martha No – Thank you – It's very . . . Clear. Christ, I – (*Laughs a little perhaps.*)

Jon I hope it's not too much of a bombardment?

Martha I don't suppose you have any cigarettes do you?

Jon takes out a packet of cigarettes, offers one to Martha. Martha takes a cigarette and Jon lights it. Beat.

Do you mind?

Jon Not only do I not mind, I might even join you.

Martha and Jon smoke.

Martha I'm trying to give up.

Jon Have you tried those e-cigarettes?

Martha I haven't.

Jon Are you alright, Martha?

Martha I think so.

Patricia You have a son.

Martha (*bit drunk*) What?

Patricia You. You have a son.

Martha Who says?

Patricia Don't fuck around.

Martha I'm sorry.

Patricia Don't fuck around and make jokes.

Martha I'm sorry, I'm sorry. Yes. I have a son. I am mother.

Patricia Fuck's sake, Martha.

Martha His name's Ben.

Patricia How old is he?

Martha Why does that matter?

Patricia I don't know but for some reason it does.

Martha Is it better if he's younger or older?

Patricia Nothing makes it better.

Martha How do you know?

Patricia Greg.

Martha Who the fuck is Greg . . . ?

Patricia The guy who you told you were gonna break his legs, ring any bells?

Martha Actually it was his fingers, it was his fiddly fucking fingers.

Patricia Are you drunk?

Martha A bit.

Patricia Greg is a friend, do you understand?

Martha Greg is a misogynist.

Patricia I think you have a problem. I think you have a problem with drink and I think you have a problem with telling the truth.

Martha What?

Patricia And I know you don't believe in free will, but I think you seriously need to exercise a bit of, like, self-fucking-control.

Martha I'm sorry, I'm sorry, 'self-control'? Do you have any idea – No, you know what, when you've – when you've actually – Because I can't imagine what it must be like being you, how hard it must be being young, and brilliant, and funny, and fucking, with things actually ahead – So I'm sorry if I've had a bit to drink and I'm sorry if I lied to you but I'm afraid the truth is, the real truth is, I don't know anything about it, I don't know anything about anything, and I have to look these patients and these people and their families, while they babble on and on and on, I have to look at them, in the eyes, in the eyes, and I have to tell them it's going to be alright – But really what I wanna say is, what I really wanna say is: we're pointless. We are pointless. We're a blip. A blip within a blip within an abyss. So, yes, I have had a bit to drink because, otherwise, frankly, I think I'd be tempted to drive a fucking hammer through my head.

Patricia (*beat*) I literally don't even know what to say to that.

Martha . . .

Patricia I'd like you to leave.

Martha That's fair enough. That was probably a bit much.

Patricia It was.

Martha I think you're amazing, Patricia, and I'm sorry I lied to you.

Patricia Yeah.

Martha I mean it, I think you're amazing.

Michael Hey, buddy, how's it going? Good news –

Harvey Not too good, actually.

Michael Oh.

Harvey I read your article.

Michael What'd you think?

Harvey Who the hell do you think you are –

Michael Whoa, Doc –

Harvey Reportage; are you kidding me?!

Michael Doc, take it easy.

Harvey You have embarrassed me – You have embarrassed my *family* –

Michael Okay, Doc, you need to –

Harvey I had a call, I had a call from my son, my son Robert –

Michael Doc –

Harvey Elouise is, is, is, inconsolable –

Michael I'm sorry to –

Harvey What does any of what happened between –

Michael Okay, look –

Harvey What does any of what happened with me and you have to do with Elouise?

Michael Doc, you're missing the p—

Harvey She is an extraordinary human being, whom I loved, whom I loved, Michael, you understand that, and you have reduced her to –

Harvey Can you please stop shouting at me for, like –

Harvey It is BS, Michael. It is a joke. A joke. You've turned this whole, this whole thing into a, into a –

Michael Can I please –

Harvey A freak show, you turned it into a freak show.

Michael In what universe is you carting around some dead guy's brain in the trunk of your car not –

Harvey You son of a bitch, it is my life!

Michael Oh gimme a – Where's the proof? Huh, Doc? Where's the evidence, where's this hallowed research –

Harvey The reason . . . The reason we haven't published, yet, is because –

Michael Doc, Jesus Christ, admit it: you got it wrong. You made – You took some guy's brain – You went, okay, gee, maybe there's something in this –

Harvey You are a liar.

Michael Yeah, well, you're deluded, so.

Harvey There is not one ounce of truth –

Michael Truth, you wanna talk about truth? How about the fact you met some guy once, *once*, Doc – you drained his piss and then you cut him open and you stole his fuckin' brain, and then, *then*, you had the nerve to act like some –

Harvey I did not –

Michael Evelyn was right, Doc: leave it the hell alone.

Harvey You have –

Michael Move on.

Harvey We had a deal!

Michael Yes, we did. And I stuck to that deal. I paid for the gas and I got you a meetin' with Evelyn.

Harvey You lied. You lied to me.

Michael Yeah, well, maybe I did. Maybe I did. But you lied to yourself, and I dunno which is worse.

Beat.

You shoulda just let the fucking thing be cremated.

Martha Hello Henry.

Henry Hello.

Martha I'm Martha.

Henry Hello Martha.

Martha How are you?

Henry I'm waiting for Margaret. Margaret and I are newlyweds.

Martha Congratulations.

Henry Thank you. We're going to London.

Martha I'm from London.

Henry We haven't met before have we?

Martha We've not, no.

Henry I wasn't sure. I have trouble remembering things, you see.

Martha I see.

Henry I'm waiting for an operation. Once that's all done and dusted, Margaret and I will be able to take our honeymoon.

Martha Do you know where?

Henry Brighton. Margaret wants to visit the West Pier. She wants to see the starlings. The formations. I don't suppose I might be able to trouble you for a cigarette?

Martha Is that allowed?

Henry I think so.

Martha lights a cigarette for Henry; lights a cigarette for herself.

(*Beat.*) Hello. Martha?

Jon He's, um. Henry, I'd like to introduce you to someone: this is Martha.

Henry Hello Martha.

Martha Hello Henry.

Henry I'm waiting for Margaret.

Martha Yes.

Henry Margaret and I are newlyweds.

Martha Congratulations.

Henry Thank you. We're going to London.

Martha Yes.

Henry We haven't met before have we?

Martha Um, we have. Actually we have.

Henry I'm sorry. I have trouble remembering things, you see.

Martha Yes.

Henry I'm waiting for an operation. Once that's all done and dusted, Margaret and I will be able to take our honeymoon.

Martha Do you know where?

Henry Brighton. Margaret wants to visit the West Pier. She wants to see the starlings. The formations.

Martha Henry, um. There's something I wanted to speak to you about, if that's alright.

Henry Please.

Martha Okay.

Beat. Martha can't quite manage to say it, to explain why she's here to see Henry. She grows upset.

Henry Hello.

Martha (*beginning to pull herself together, as it were*)
Hello Henry.

Henry Here –

He offers Martha his handkerchief.

Martha Thank you, Henry.

Henry We haven't met before have we?

Martha We have. But don't worry.

Henry I have trouble remembering things, you see.

Martha Don't worry. Henry?

Henry Yes.

Martha Jon tells me you're a bit of a pianist?

Henry I don't know.

Martha My son's a musician. I'd love to hear you play.
If you didn't mind.

Henry Alright.

He moves to the piano and takes a seat. Beat.

What do you want me to play?

Martha I don't mind. Whatever you want.

*Beat. Henry plays the melody taught to him by
Margaret. He plays with great confidence and fluidity;
it's fucking brilliant.*